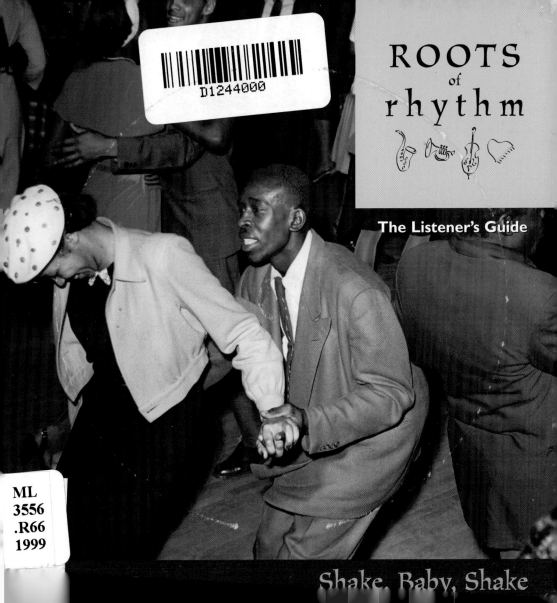

ROOTS
of
rhythm

The Listener's Guide

Shake, Baby, Shake

Shake, Baby, Shake

Rhythm, as basic to life as the heartbeat, is the root of all music—
and this first volume of Roots of Rhythm has a beat that just won't
quit. "Shake, Baby, Shake" includes 1940s jumpin' classics that
made rock 'n' roll possible, like Louis Jordan's "Choo Choo
Ch'Boogie," as well as early rock hits like Little Richard's "Tutti-
Frutti." Along the way, there's the first fuzz-tone guitar (in Jackie
Brenston's "Rocket '88'") and the original singing bartender (Big
Joe Turner belting out "Shake, Rattle and Roll"). Call it blues,
swing, rock or boogie-woogie, "Shake Baby Shake" is a heart-
pounder. And as Cab Calloway might say, that's no hi-de-ho.

The Listener's Guide: What the Symbols Mean

Infusions
The musician's
influences and
inspiration

The Sound
Style, structure
and subtleties
explained

Music Maker
The musician's
life—the good
times and the
hardships

Time & Place
Circumstances
and events that
shaped the music

Table of Contents

Shake, Rattle and Roll

Rhythm & Blues
Big Joe Turner

The sheer power of Big Joe Turner's booming baritone comes at you loud and clear in his biggest hit, "Shake, Rattle and Roll." This was the No. 1 rhythm & blues song of 1954, topping the charts for three weeks. Yet it was more than that. In this song, Big Joe gives you a glimpse of the future of rock 'n' roll. The rolling rhythm of the saxophones, the hand-clappin' beat and Big Joe's irresistible voice get you up out of your chair and onto the dance floor. That was the essence of rhythm & blues and of early rock 'n' roll, and few sang it better than Big Joe Turner.

KEY NOTES

If you like Big Joe, check out these artists:
- Elvis Presley
- Big Bill Broonzy
- Jimmy Rushing
- Pete Johnson
- Louis Jordan
- Smiley Lewis

Big Daddy of Rock 'n' Roll

Soon after "Shake, Rattle and Roll" was released, Bill Haley and the Comets (right) recorded their version of the song, which catapulted to No. 7 on the rock 'n' roll charts. The tune not only made an instant star of Bill Haley, it influenced much of his music and that of other early rockers, including Elvis Presley, who also recorded the song. The significance of Big Joe's music was never lost on Haley, who idolized Turner. The two musicians became close friends and their bands even toured together—despite protests and threats from racists who felt that white and black bands shouldn't appear on the same stage.

The Kansas City Sound

Turner was greatly influenced by the blues and jazz artists who came through his hometown of Kansas City in the 1930s. At that time, the proliferation of nightclubs (as well as gambling and bootlegging) made Kansas City a hotbed for musical talent. Big, swinging jazz bands led by Count Basie and Bennie Moten played the larger clubs, while blues shouters and ragtime bands worked the smaller clubs.

These diverse sounds eventually came together in a boogie-woogie style—music structured in the blues' eight- and 12-bar form, but with saxophones, instrumental solos and a swing beat mixed in. Turner and his friend, pianist Pete Johnson (left), led the way in this genre, creating "up-tempo" danceable blues. Their music ignited a boogie-woogie craze, and later evolved into rhythm & blues.

You Can't Say That

The lyrics of "Shake, Rattle and Roll" were a little too bawdy for 1950s pop radio stations. Provocative lines such as "wearin' those dresses, the sun comes shinin' through/I can't believe my eyes, all that mess belongs to you..." kept Turner's tune from receiving widespread airplay. Knowing this, Bill Haley's producer had the words changed for his band. In Haley's version you hear, "Wearin' those dresses, your hair's done up so nice/you look so warm, but your heart's as cold as ice."

SHAKE RATTLE AND ROLL

The Singing Bartender

Joe Turner's rich, bluesy voice was so clear and powerful that he could sing without a microphone and be heard over a 12-piece band. This particular talent helped him get noticed while working as a bartender at Kansas City's Sunset Cafe. While mixing drinks, Turner would hear his cue for a song and start belting out the

blues from behind the bar. With accompaniment from pianist Pete Johnson, the joint would soon be jumpin'. It was at the Sunset that Turner was first heard by jazz impresario John Hammond, who invited him and Johnson to perform at Carnegie Hall, in a 1938 concert billed Spirituals to Swing. A week after the concert, they were recording their first songs, on the Vocalion label.

Choo Choo Ch'Boogie

Boogie-Woogie

Louis Jordan and His Tympany Five

Alto sax man Louis Jordan's famous shuffle beat takes center stage in "Choo Choo Ch'Boogie," a million-seller in 1946 that rode the rails all the way to No. 1 on the R&B chart and No. 7 on the pop list. Jordan, who caught a one-way train from his native Arkansas to Philadelphia during the Depression, celebrates the syncopation of wheels on steel. The drums lock in and the cymbals accent the four-four beat. The lyrics—"listen to the rhythm of the clickety-clack...hang around with Democratic fellas named Mack"—recall a time before air travel that already felt nostalgic a year after World War II.

KEY NOTES

If you like Louis Jordan, check out these artists:

- Chick Webb
- Percy Mayfield
- Buddy Johnson
- James Brown
- Joe Liggins and His Honeydrippers
- Amos Milburn

The Jump Boogie Renaissance

Its fans may not know it, but today's so-called "swing" revival—in nightclubs like the Brown Derby in Los Angeles and in the style of bands like the Squirrel Nut Zippers—is misnamed. There's little swing jazz in the music of today's zoot suit-wearing hepcats. It is, in fact, a jump renaissance—and the roots of the modern swingsters' music is pure Tympany Five. It honks and wiggles just like Jordan's stuff, and the guys even dress like Jordan—only not as well. Jordan died in 1975—perhaps despondent that the only dance craze then was disco.

The Demise of the Big Bands

The big bands of the 1930s (like Duke Ellington's, below) were gloriously excessive, but if the World War II economy didn't do them in, the fast-forward postwar culture made them seem anachronistic. Jordan started as a saxophonist in Chick Webb's big band in the late '30s but was "downsized" and turned to his own group, the Tympany Five. Unlike big bands with their multiple horns, small combos featured only one of each instrument. With less structure, musicians had

more freedom to play off the beat—juicing the rhythm in what came to be known as jump boogie, and then rhythm & blues. Jordan's small combo influenced many fledgling R&B groups, but one important link to big band jazz remained: his own florid alto playing.

Out of the Hospital, into the Studio

"Choo Choo Ch'Boogie" was one of the first Top 40 hits Jordan recorded after being hospitalized in the mid-'40s. Jordan was a huge star in the African-American community, and the black press from coast to coast had been full of news of how the bandleader's wife, Fleecie (his third of five wives), attacked him in bed with a toenail clipper, nearly cutting off several fingers. His sax playing on "Choo Choo Ch'Boogie," however, sounds just fine. The song offers proof that despite his showy style, Jordan was also a fine instrumentalist, with technique that was widely respected by more "serious" jazz musicians, including the emerging beboppers.

Long Before MTV

Jordan, who began as a song-and-dance man on the vaudeville stage, was a consummate showman, who recognized the visual potential of pop music back when most so-called swing artists were glued to their chairs. He delighted in appearing in light musical films, such as *Follow the Boys*, *Sweet Miss Bobby Sox* and *Swing Parade of 1946* (above). More significantly in retrospect, he filmed short clips in the 1940s that could be considered the original music videos—and are available on video today.

Calloway Boogie
Swing
Cab Calloway

In the mid-1940s a raft of piano-stoked boogie-woogie tunes were climbing the charts, and big-band leader Cab Calloway, ever on the lookout for a trend, smoothly adapted that small-combo sound for his late-1947 recording "Calloway Boogie." Here the translation to a big-band sound, fueled by His Hi-De-Ho Highness of Jive's scat acrobatics, seems purely natural. Although the song never made the charts, it demonstrates why Calloway was able to stay near the top for decades; when he seized on a new sound—whether it was jive, bebop or a waltz—he made it his own.

A Sportin' Life

Calloway played Sportin' Life (right), the been-there, done-that good-timer in George Gershwin's *Porgy and Bess*. The celebrated 1950 Broadway show helped resurrect his career, which had stalled after his hits of the '40s. The fun-loving bandleader did not have to stretch much for the role. In fact, Gershwin had modeled the character on Calloway, a man who knew how to live. When he was a teenager, Calloway's parents shipped him off to a special school because he was hanging out too much at the Pimlico racetrack in Baltimore. He ended up being the first black man allowed into the stands at Hialeah and the first to perform at the Preakness. All his life he was a gambler—whether it was on an unknown filly at Aqueduct or on a new vocal at the Cotton Club.

The Hi-De-Ho Man

Whether Calloway was in vaudeville, at the Cotton Club in Harlem or on Broadway, he was an outstanding, and outstandingly shameless, singer. One minute he could be heart-wrenchingly clear, and in the very next he was making a mockery of things, playing to the cheap seats. His love of gibberish shows in a song like "Calloway Boogie," where he ends up scatting his classic "Hi-De-Ho" line. He claimed he discovered this style one night when he forgot the lyrics; others suggest he borrowed from the Spirits of Rhythm's Leo Watson. In any case, the Hi-De-Ho Man ended up making scat his signature sound.

The Black Vaudeville Circuit

Calloway came out of vaudeville, the anything-goes variety shows that were the most popular form of entertainment in America before radio and movies. Vaudeville was carefully segregated, and the black "circuits"—the term used to describe a chain of theaters through which performers traveled—were grueling tours of duty. The shows sparkled, but there was little glamour behind the scenes, just cheap hotels and grinding schedules. Calloway, who in the 1920s sang in a famous revue called *Plantation Days*, worked the TOBA (Theatre Owners and Bookers

Association) circuit, a Deep South chain of music houses owned by whites but located in black neighborhoods. The road-weary performers joked that TOBA stood for Tough On Black Asses.

The Calloway Style

Calloway's imposing zoot suits (at right) helped introduce the style to mainstream America. But his outrageous fashion sense went beyond '40s fashion to influence stage costumes worn by stars like Elvis, James Brown and David Byrne—even the white three-piece suit worn by John Travolta in *Saturday Night Fever*. And check out the latest threads on hip hopper Puffy Combs: Those big suits and metallic ties look very Calloway.

Track 4

Jim Dandy
Rhythm & Blues
LaVern Baker

With its frantic cry "Jim Dandy to the rescue!" LaVern Baker's biggest hit rings with a comic-book intensity. The taut rhythm and vaguely suggestive lyrics ("Jim Dandy he's the kinda guy/ Never likes to see a little girl cry") made the song both sexy and silly. It was a dandy formula for a teen hit in 1956; "Jim Dandy" rose to No. 1 on the R&B chart and also hit No. 17 on the pop list. By applying her gospel-tinged vocals to rowdy adolescent themes, Baker was a pioneer of rock 'n' roll. She followed up this hit with "Jim Dandy Got Married," a No. 7 R&B seller in 1957.

KEY NOTES

If you like
LaVern Baker,
check out:
- Jackie Wilson
- Ruth Brown
- Esther Phillips
- Wanda Jackson
- Memphis Minnie
- Bessie Smith

A Dandy Idea

Baker's music appealed equally to blacks and whites, but that didn't stop white artists from rerecording her hits. Jazz chanteuse Georgia Gibbs recorded numerous staid cover versions of Baker songs (much to the annoyance of Baker herself). And in 1974, the Southern hard rock band Black Oak Arkansas (right) had a Top 30 hit with their version of "Jim Dandy." In live shows the band's lead singer, "Jim Dandy" Mangrum, and a female counterpart improvised lewd lyrics to the song that would have made '50s teenagers blush.

Alan Freed and Early TV

Alan Freed, one of the first white disc jockeys to play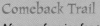
black music in the '50s, recognized Baker as one of
rock 'n' roll's early stars. Freed was a celebrity in his own
right, with popular radio shows in Cleveland and New York.
While he helped many black artists gain stature, he helped himself to
enormous power before his career was ruined by a record-industry
bribery scandal in the early 1960s. In his heyday, Freed put Baker in

two movies (*Rock, Rock, Rock*, left, and *Mr. Rock 'n' Roll*), featured her on his radio shows and took her on the road in his revue. Baker was also a pioneer of lip-synching—making regular appearances on Dick Clark's *Philadelphia Bandstand*.

Little Miss Sharecropper

Born Delores Williams, Baker started singing novelty tunes in 1946 as Little Miss Sharecropper, wearing a tattered sack dress and performing at the Club de Lisa in her native Chicago. As LaVern Baker, she later recorded R&B hits such as "Tweedlee Dee," "Tra-La-La" and "Humpty Dumpty Heartbreak."

"Jim Dandy," based on a mythic folk hero dating back to the 19th century, was just one in a long line of Baker songs with silly lyrics based on nursery rhymes and children's literature (original sheet music pictured above).

Comeback Trail

After performing for troops in Vietnam, Baker retired in 1969 to the Philippines, where she spent 20 years as entertainment director at a U.S. military base. She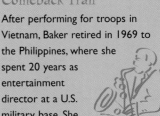
returned to America in 1990 to replace her old Atlantic label mate Ruth Brown in the Broadway revue *Black & Blue* (she stayed nine months) and hit the

nightclub circuit in major U.S. cities. That same year, she sang "Slow Rollin' Mama" on the *Dick Tracy* motion picture soundtrack. She was inducted into both the R&B and Rock and Roll halls of fame, and performed practically until her death in 1997, despite having lost both her legs as a result of diabetes in the '90s.

The Twist

Rhythm & Blues

Hank Ballard and the Midnighters

Hank Ballard and the Midnighters' original, raucous 1959 recording of "The Twist" is most famous for what it wasn't. For starters, it wasn't about a dance craze (that notion was invented a year later, to promote Chubby Checker's cover version), although anyone who could resist dancing to this number was probably dead. It also wasn't a hit at the time. But with bristling, brilliant guitar work, tight church harmonies yearning to roll in the dirt, and a screaming front man, the original "Twist" is clearly the real thing, even if it took others to turn the T-word into a teen sensation.

Motor City Melting Pot

Postwar Detroit, where Ballard grew up, was flooded with both black and white Southerners—as well as Central European immigrants —who had come to work in the munitions and auto factories. Ballard himself worked on the assembly line when he was 15. A relatively integrated one-industry town where blacks and whites worked side by side and made decent union wages, Detroit became a cultural melting pot where Ballard could absorb all kinds of music—he was a big fan of cowboy crooner Gene Autry.

New Twist on an Old Tune

While the Midnighters were more than once condemned in church, "The Twist" was actually born there. Taking the melody of a gospel hymn, the vocal group the Drifters composed "What'cha Gonna Do?" in 1955. Two years later, Ballard (right) and the Midnighters rerecorded that song as "Is Your

Love Real?" A year after that, Ballard added suggestive lyrics vaguely about dancing, rearranged the instruments and put it on the B-side of a soft ballad called "Teardrops on Your Letter." "The Midnighters invented the Twist," Ballard once said. "I was just watching [the band] go through their routines, seeing them twisting their bodies, and the lyric just came to me—*twist*." The song was the first to include Ballard's name on the label in front of the Midnighters. They went on to create several other dance-themed hits, such as "The Continental Walk" and "The Float."

Chubby Checker and the Dance Craze

Dick Clark wanted to book the Midnighters on *American Bandstand*, but when they couldn't make it, he got a former chicken-plucker named Chubby Checker to sing it—and dance it—instead. A career and a craze were made; the song became a No. 1 hit in 1960 for Checker. Some of his success then rubbed off on the Midnighters, who saw their version reach No. 28 on the pop chart after Chubby's hit.

Sex Sells

Midnighter hits from the early '50s, such as "Get It," "Sexy Ways," "Work with Me Annie" and "Open Up Your Back Door," didn't need a whole lot of explanation. But R&B's audience was growing, and when young white fans began singing the suggestive lyrics in the shower,

parents were outraged. "Work with Me Annie" became one of the first pop music scandals—and Ballard shrewdly recognized the commercial value in scandal. In 1974, he cut a record called "Let's Go Streaking," which he recorded, so it is said, in the nude.

Johnny B. Goode
Rock 'n' Roll
Chuck Berry

Rock 'n' roll was already here to stay by the time Chuck Berry's 1958 No. 8 hit "Johnny B. Goode" sent teenagers across America into air-guitar heaven. But his single-string and double-stop playing style—with note-bending melodies as expressive as the human voice—made it official: The guitar was to be the instrument of rock, and nobody's style was more imitated than Berry's. The song's lyrics, about a poor guitar picker's rise to fame, also made "Johnny B. Goode" the first rock tune about being a rock star. Little wonder this rock original has become an oldies radio classic.

Good Humor Man

Chuck Berry did three stints in prison in three different decades (for armed robbery in the '40s, a morals charge in the '60s and tax evasion in the '70s). These experiences left Berry feeling bitter and aloof, yet those emotions never crept into his music, and his fans never left him. In fact, while in prison in the '60s, he penned "Nadine," "You Never Can Tell" and "No Particular Place to Go"—Top 30 hits in the U.S. and U.K. "Everything I wrote wasn't about me," Berry (right, with British fans) once said, "but about the people listening to [me]."

Here's Johnny!

The title character in "Johnny B. Goode" was inspired by Berry's rollicking piano player—and longtime friend—Johnnie Johnson (below, right). And the lyric about how "that little country boy could play" was originally written as "colored boy." Berry changed it for commercial reasons: He knew that the line would brand the song as "race music" and diminish its chances of ever getting played on pop radio. Ultimately, of course, Johnny is none other than Berry himself. As he said in his 1987 autobiography, "I wrote

of a boy with an ambition to become a guitar player, who came from the least of luxury to be seen by many, practicing until the listener believes he has all but made it to the top as the chorus prompts him like his mother's encouraging voice, 'Go Johnny Go!'"

A Synthesizing Student

The influences on Berry's guitar style couldn't be more diverse. There is the ringing single-note style of jazz guitarist Charlie Christian (right), the electricity that crackled in the playing of Carl Hogan (from the Louis Jordan band), and then there are the spontaneous, dazzlingly phrased solos of T-Bone Walker. He listened to their songs and retooled their techniques in a way that wasn't jazz or the blues, but only rock 'n' roll.

Fresh Breeze in the Windy City

Chuck Berry owes his first big break to Muddy Waters. The blues legend introduced Chicago record label owner Leonard Chess to Berry, a young man from East St. Louis with lightning guitar licks, brilliantly clear vocals and a headful of wry, catchy songs. Chess Records, where Berry recorded "Johnny B. Goode" and all his early hits, had made its

name in the early '50s as a sanctuary of serious blues— the place where transplanted southerners, such as Howlin' Wolf and Muddy himself, established themselves as icons. Berry's teen-targeted music turned Chess from blues mecca to the baptismal font of rock 'n' roll.

Got My Mojo Working

Blues
Muddy Waters

Muddy Waters' 1956 recording of "Got My Mojo
Working" worked like a charm—it became one of
his signature songs, and a classic of the Chicago
blues. The harmonica, formerly a background
instrument in country blues, is played in the
recording through an amplifier. In the hand of Little
Walter Jacobs it has all the presence of a booming
saxophone. The big wall of up-tempo blues sound is
perfect for the powerful voice of Waters, who used
the song to close his live performances—and keep
the audience workin' to his beat all the way home.

The Maxwell Street Market

Chicago's South Side was the last stop for
thousands of blacks who had moved north from
the Mississippi Delta after World War II. By the
early '50s the neighborhood's bustling streets
were lined with blues clubs like Pepper's,
Sylvio's and Smitty's Corner. But one of the main venues for up-
and-coming musicians was the famous open-air market on
Maxwell Street. There, future greats like Muddy Waters and
Robert Nighthawk performed for coins on Saturday afternoons.
Mick Jagger made a pilgrimage to the market in the 1970s, and
scenes for the 1980 film *Blues Brothers* were shot there.

Mojo, Defined

A "mojo" or "mojo hand" is a voodoo charm, often kept in a flannel purse and worn around the neck or waist, most common in Southern locales like Louisiana, where Muddy learned this song while touring. Originating in African and Caribbean folklore, mojos were meant to ward off evil spirits or bring good luck. They could be roots, bones, precious stones, feathers, herbs, even dried frogs or bats' wings. While the guitarist may not personally have ascribed to voodoo magic, he recognized the power in the lyric's sexual innuendo—and he wasn't first. A 1930s blues song by Coot Grant and Kid Socks called "Take Your Hands Off My Mojo" featured a risqué duet. Much later, in their hit "L.A. Woman," The Doors sang about "Mr. Mojo risin'"—which was an anagram for "Jim Morrison."

The Brits Missed a Beat

Muddy Waters greatly influenced early British rock bands such as the Stones, the Yardbirds (including Keith Relf, below center) and the Animals. But when he first toured England in 1958, locals expected to hear acoustic Southern blues, not electrified songs like "Hoochie Coochie Man" and "Got My Mojo Working," which he had been recording in Chicago. British critics blasted the shows: "Screaming Guitar and Howling Piano" was not a compliment. When Waters

returned in 1962, a friend took him to a London nightclub featuring a blues rock band so loud that it hurt Muddy's ears. By then British fans had completely soaked up Muddy's electric blues sound.

The Librarian and the Sharecropper

When Muddy Waters first recorded in 1941, he was a sharecropper on a Mississippi plantation. He played and sang at weekend fish fries and rural juke joints; to earn a little extra money, he also bootlegged whiskey. When Waters was approached by a representative of the Library of Congress to record for a series on American folk music, he suspected that the man was a revenuer looking for his whiskey still. But the librarian won Muddy's trust by drinking water after him, from the same cup.

Hound Dog
Rhythm & Blues
Big Mama Thornton

Willie Mae Thornton's opening vocal cry on "Hound Dog" leaves no doubt why she was called Big Mama. In this original 1953 version of a song that became a rock 'n' roll standard, Thornton reaches into the pit of her soul to growl a searing indictment of a no-good man. Although the song later became a much bigger hit for a certain hip-swiveling guy from Tupelo, Thornton's recording stands on its own. Reflecting in its improvisational feel the influence of jazz music as well as the new sound of electric blues, her recording was the No. 1 R&B hit for seven weeks.

Traveling Band

Big Mama Thornton's father was a minister in Alabama, and she was raised singing in his church. She learned both drums and harmonica by her teens, but a life of prayer had little hold on her; when she was 14 she snuck off with Sammy Green's Hot Harlem Revue, touring the country. Settling later in Houston, she met club owner Don Robey, who also ran the Peacock and Duke record labels. She signed a deal with him and went on the road with Robey's house bandleader Johnny Otis and His Rhythm & Blues Caravan. Otis was also a prolific producer during the early '50s, and he got the idea to record "Hound Dog" during the caravan's stopover in Los Angeles. Big Mama (right, with Curtis Tillman's Band) belted out the hit, and then she hit the road again.

Every Dog Has His Day

Even though "Hound Dog" producer and bandleader Johnny Otis (above) led a large orchestra, he knew that the song would have more power with fewer instruments. Using just bass, guitar and drums—the instrumentation that would soon become the core of rock 'n' roll—he laid a spare foundation that left Big Mama Thornton plenty of room to fill. Guitarist Pete Lewis provided a legendary backup that sounds just as mean as Mama's voice. And those voices barking like dogs at the end? That's the rest of his band, making themselves useful while hanging around the studio.

Elvis Presley's Howler

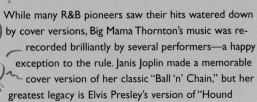

While many R&B pioneers saw their hits watered down by cover versions, Big Mama Thornton's music was re-recorded brilliantly by several performers—a happy exception to the rule. Janis Joplin made a memorable cover version of her classic "Ball 'n' Chain," but her greatest legacy is Elvis Presley's version of "Hound Dog"—a song written by the composer/producers Jerry Leiber and Mike Stoller. Recorded in New York just four years after Thornton's R&B version, Presley's rockabilly interpretation became a million-seller and one of the King's signature songs. Unfortunately, the song was also at the center of one of early rock's most embarrassing moments: On the Steve Allen TV show in 1956, Elvis was forced to croon the song to a basset hound named Sherlock.

One Cool Cat

Rufus Thomas (below), then a popular disc jockey and nightclub entertainer in Memphis, heard Big Mama shooing the hound dog from her door and decided to

record an "answer record"—the polite term for cashing in on a hit—called "Bear Cat." It used the same tune and arrangement as "Hound Dog" but replaced the words with his. It became the first hit for Sun Records.

Rocket "88"

Rhythm & Blues

Jackie Brenston
and His Delta Cats

"Rocket '88,'" Jackie Brenston's only hit, is driven by a loping bass and Ike Turner's rhythmic piano playing. The band was actually Ike's, Brenston was his vocalist. Willie Kizart's guitar is also brought from the rhythm section to the front of the band—itself a major innovation, but not as significant as the fuzzy, distorted sound he gets out of his instrument. "Rocket '88,'" a No. 1 R&B hit in 1951, is genuine rock 'n' roll not just in its style but also in its subject: girls and cars, in this case, the Oldsmobile Delta 88 (below).

KEY NOTES

If you like Jackie Brenston, check out these artists:

- Roscoe Gordon
- Ike & Tina Turner
- James Cotton
- Doctor Ross
- Barbara Pittman
- Junior Parker
- Link Wray

The First Fuzzy Guitar

One of the most distinctive sounds on this record is the distortion on Willie Kizart's electric guitar. Like many of the best innovations, this was an accident. On the drive up to Memphis from Clarksdale, Mississippi, the band's station wagon was overflowing, so some of the equipment was tied to the roof. On the way, Kizart's amp went tumbling, breaking the speaker cone. At the studio, they tried to patch it. The paper created a fuzzy tone, and producer Sam Phillips, instead of recoiling from the unusual sound, pushed it further, overamplifying it and building the band's sound around it.

Jackie and Ike

Ike Turner was a popular bandleader in Clarksdale, Mississippi (near Memphis). He and his singer, Jackie Brenston, heard about Sam Phillips and his Memphis Recording Service from B.B. King. Turner had worked up this rollicking car song and figured Phillips might

FIRST TIME IN MEMPHIS!
W.C. HANDY THEATRE
2 DAYS ONLY - SAT. & SUN. APRIL 7-8
ON STAGE! ----- IN PERSON

★ JACKIE BRENSTON ★
THE TERRIFIC **ROCKET "88"** SENSATION
★ WITH ★
IKE TURNER
" **THE KING OF THE PIANO** "
★—" **HIS KING OF RHYTHM** "—★
JACKIE IS GONNA TEAR THE HOUSE DOWN
ADMISSION_____ 60c Tax. Incl.

go for it. Everyone was pleased until the record came out; when Turner saw it was under Brenston's name, Ike took his band and left. Brenston assembled a new set of Delta Cats and continued to record, but with little success.

Sam Phillips and the Search for Soul

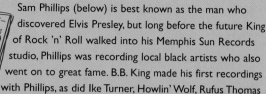

Sam Phillips (below) is best known as the man who discovered Elvis Presley, but long before the future King of Rock 'n' Roll walked into his Memphis Sun Records studio, Phillips was recording local black artists who also went on to great fame. B.B. King made his first recordings with Phillips, as did Ike Turner, Howlin' Wolf, Rufus Thomas and Junior Parker. Phillips was after the sounds they made for themselves. "I had the patience to listen to them and also let them know that there was nothing they could do that would be ridiculous, except not sing and pick for me," Phillips wrote. A keen talent scout and talented producer, Phillips played a key role in the development of rhythm & blues and rock 'n' roll. He was inducted into the Rock and Roll Hall of Fame in 1986.

A Different Effect

After "Rocket '88'," distortion became a sonic mainstay for an instrument that was rapidly taking center stage. Future guitarists (such as Stevie Ray Vaughn, left) "cranked up" their amps to get that overdriven sound, and amplifier makers eventually included a distortion knob as an effects feature.

Tutti-Frutti

Rock 'n' Roll

Little Richard

There is nothing subtle about Little Richard's music, and certainly not about "Tutti-Frutti," his first and greatest hit. From the opening scat line, "A-Wop-Bop-A-Loo-Bop, A-Lop-Bam-Boom," it's clear that this is classic rock 'n' roll. "Tutti-Frutti" races along with an incredible energy, paced by a driving brass section, powerful drum work, piano riffs and a soaring saxophone solo. Add to all this Little Richard's trademark falsettos and faintly suggestive lyrics and it's easy to see why listeners in the 1950s were quick to pick up on Little Richard's favorite expression, "Ooh, my soul!"

Liverpool Meets Macon, Georgia

Among Little Richard's greatest admirers were the stars of the British Invasion of the early 1960s, the Beatles and the Rolling Stones. After one of his brief flirtations with religion, Little Richard went to England and toured with the Beatles, then a little-known group that was developing a cult following. Many of their best early songs were covers, or remakes, of songs by Little Richard and other early rock 'n' roll stars. Indeed, the Beatles recorded no fewer than six Little Richard songs, "Tutti-Frutti" among them. Little Richard also taught the Beatles the falsetto riffs so prominent on "She Loves You (Yeah, Yeah, Yeah)" and "I Want to Hold Your Hand." Then there was the flamboyant onstage persona of the Rolling Stones' Mick Jagger. This was a pure, electrifying testimonial to Little Richard. For Jagger it was an act. For Little Richard it was art imitating life.

A True Original

There were many rhythm & blues singers with better voices than Little Richard. There were songs that were as catchy and powerful as his many hits. And there were even performers who could match his showmanship, if not his campiness and utter flamboyance. But what made Little Richard

unique was his ability to bring the entire package together with a faintly dangerous, almost devilish

edge. He was both a jester and a tempter, offering the teenagers of the 1950s a look—and an invitation—to a walk on the wild side. They loved it.

Good Golly, It's Pat Boone!

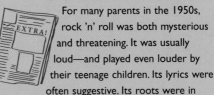

For many parents in the 1950s, rock 'n' roll was both mysterious and threatening. It was usually loud—and played even louder by their teenage children. Its lyrics were often suggestive. Its roots were in

R&B, which meant that many of its early stars were African-American at a time when discrimination was the norm. Throw in the overt campiness of Little Richard and it's clear why many adults weren't too thrilled by "Tutti-Frutti." Enter Pat Boone. He was pure vanilla, the boy next door and every mother's dream. When he sang "Tutti-Frutti," it seemed less threatening, lacking the raw energy of the original. But while Little Richard's records sold well, they were routinely outsold by Boone's. It's interesting to note that in the 1990s, when Boone, on a lark, performed as a heavy metal artist, many of his fans were outraged. Little Richard may have outraged a lot of people, but never his fans.

The Hit That Almost Wasn't

Little Richard's first and greatest hit was a fluke. Art Rupe, of Specialty Records in Los Angeles, was looking for a Ray Charles soundalike and brought Little Richard to New Orleans for a recording session.

The session was going badly until, during a break, Little Richard impulsively broke into "Tutti-Frutti," a sexually suggestive song he created, possibly on the spur of the moment. Rupe loved it, ordered the lyrics cleaned up and released it just before Christmas 1955. It became a hit almost overnight and Little Richard was on his way to stardom.

Bo Diddley
Rock 'n' Roll
Bo Diddley

Bo Diddley blew in from nowhere in 1955 to create one of rock's defining sounds. His self-titled debut song, a No. 1 pop hit, introduced a brand-new mix of African percussion, gospel and country. Diddley's heavily distorted electric guitar, the surging "shave-and-a-haircut-six-bits" beat and an exotic maracas backup sounded like nothing else. Though each musician seems to be playing a different rhythm, the ensemble is tight and unrelenting. The song's title itself was a bit of self-promotion, but in hindsight, appropriate—having launched the career of a rock pioneer.

KEY NOTES

If you like Bo Diddley, check out these other artists:

- Ray Charles
- Jackie Wilson
- Little Richard
- Buddy Holly and the Crickets

Bo Breaks Big, and Fast

EXTRA!

Shortly after being signed to Chess Records' Checker label in 1955, Diddley's boastful calling card "Bo Diddley" leapt to the top of the R&B chart in just two months, and his other debut single, "I'm A Man," became a much-covered hit. Right away the former busker was touring and playing a number of big shows, including Dr. Jive's R&B Revue at the Apollo, Alan Freed's Diddley Daddy R&B package show and Ed Sullivan's *Toast of the Town*, where he played his signature song "Bo Diddley." He also gigged at Carnegie Hall.

What's in a Name?

Bo Diddley is a man of many names. He was born Otha Ellas Bates in McComb, Mississippi, but was soon adopted by his mother's cousin, Gussie McDaniel, and took their last name, moving with them to Chicago during the Depression. Somewhere along the line he lost his original first name and became known as Ellas McDaniel. Although the

artist has claimed "Bo Diddley" is slang for "bully" and was given him on the playground, others insist he got the name as an amateur boxer. Coincidentally, in Bo's native Mississippi, a "diddley bow" is the name of a children's one-stringed instrument on which is often played that same "shave-and-a-haircut-six-bits" rhythm popularized by Bo (left, with his band in Chicago).

Buddy and Bo

Diddley popularized a guitar effect called "tremolo," a choppy mock-echo sound created electronically that was appropriated by Buddy Holly (left) in hits like "Not Fade Away." Holly, like Diddley, had learned violin as a child before switching to guitar, and he was equally savvy in the studio. Diddley's tremolo technique and his distinctive bouncing "shave-and-a-haircut-six-bits" rhythm live on in Holly's classic hits, as well as in remakes like The Rolling Stones' version of "Not Fade Away."

If You Got It, Shout It

"Bo Diddley" was the first of many Diddley tunes to incorporate the singsong, boastful chanting he had picked up in schoolyards as a child. Often called "the dozens" (these days it's called "dissing"), the lyrics usually featured forms of one-upmanship, often concerning sexual prowess. Bo had an able foil in his maracas player, Jerome Green (below, right), with whom he would sometimes share lead vocals and exchange good-natured insults on record. The pair had been playing together— and giving each other the dozens— since the early 1950s, when they had a sidewalk group called the Langley Avenue Jive Cats.

Papa's Got a Brand New Bag

Funk

James Brown

"This is a hit!" James Brown shouted at the beginning of the 1965 recording session for "Papa's Got a Brand New Bag." And he was right. Brown's first Top 10 record was well titled, as it introduced a brand-new sound that would come to be known as funk. In "Bag," bandleader Brown makes every instrument a messenger of the rhythm. Horns, guitars, keyboards and drums explode with precision on the same beat. It was all about the pulse. This wasn't a band, it was a drum—and Brown was banging it loudly.

He Aimed to Please

James Brown has lived a life onstage, sliding across it on his knees, begging us "Please, Please, Please." But Brown never went begging when it came to business. He was a shrewd money man who combined the street smarts he learned in a Georgia reform school with innate marketing savvy. Recognizing the power of his live performances, he toured incessantly—and made sure local radio stations and record stores were stocked with his recordings before arriving in town. He also printed upcoming tour dates on his record covers—now a common marketing tie-in, but in the early '60s a brand-new bag, indeed.

"You Just Kind of Take It and Move It"

When James Brown recorded "Papa's Got a Brand New Bag," he was returning to the studio after an 11-month hiatus while feuding with the King label. In that time he'd turned his music upside down. In "Bag" you hear Brown moving away from the blues-based structure of his previous hits "Please, Please, Please" and "Night Train," and incorporating syncopation and open-ended vamps. Among the innovations of "Papa's Got a Brand New Bag" were the contrasting rhythms of the horns and the guitars, the offbeat bass lines, and the fact that the rhythm was "on the one," meaning the beat was accented

on the first and third notes instead of the second and fourth notes. "When I recorded 'Papa's Got a Brand New Bag,' that was a new formula to music," Brown declared. "Jazz licks with a gospel overtone—which has no musical concept where you can actually write it. You just kind of take it and move it." America moved with it.

Brown Takes the T.A.M.I. Show

Around the same time "Papa's Got a Brand New Bag" became Brown's breakthrough hit, he crawled across the stage into America's living rooms on a TV revue known as the T.A.M.I. (Teen Age Music International) Show. Brown saw his moment and blew away the other performers—including the Rolling Stones, Chuck Berry and Marvin Gaye. His I-can't-leave-the-stage-alive finale (Brown drops to the floor repeatedly before his valet drags him away) is captured in all its glory.

Father of Funk

The one-chord explosions that James Brown set off in "Brand New Bag" paved the way for a whole generation of funk bands, and in the case of Parliament/Funkadelic, the influence couldn't have been more direct. Several members of George Clinton's P-Funk band of the early '70s came from Brown's backing bands, including bass player Bootsy Collins (above), legendary saxophonist Maceo Parker (who's featured on "Brand New Bag") and trombonist Fred Wesley.

Land of 1,000 Dances
Soul
Wilson Pickett

When it comes to high-energy soul songs, Wilson Pickett's 1966 "Land of 1,000 Dances" sets the standard. The rhythm works up from the feet into a non-stop hip-shaking assault. On his first Top 10 pop hit, Wicked Pickett is a pistol, the band an arsenal of dance grooves. "Help me!" Pickett screams, and the band takes it personally—the guitar percolates, and the horns beat out the rhythm like drums. A milestone in the style that came to be known as Southern soul, "Land of 1,000 Dances" was a hit that no one could take sitting down.

From Cotton Fields to Back Alleys

As a teenager, Pickett moved from Alabama to Detroit, where his father lived, because his mother felt the brash child needed more discipline. The move from cotton fields to street corners didn't exactly turn Pickett into a choirboy, but "a lot of messin' around and singin' in Detroit alleys" did expose him to a much broader range of musical styles. In the 1950s the

young singer became steeped in the sidewalk sounds of doo-wop groups, such as the Moonglows, the Dominoes and the Drifters (above), who used gospel harmonies not in the praise of God but of women—a subject Wilson could definitely relate to. Pickett, in fact, had his own vocal group, the Falcons, from 1961 to '63 before going solo.

His Wicked Ways

Wilson's nickname, Wicked Pickett, was part marketing ploy and part accurate description. Legend has it that on a visit to Atlantic Records' New York office in 1966, Pickett pinched the posterior of a secretary, who yelled out "God, you sure are wicked!" Hearing that, producer Jerry Wexler (below, right) said, "That's his next album—*The Wicked Pickett!*"

Bible Belter

Pickett, one of 11 siblings in a family of Alabama sharecroppers, had a preacher grandfather who had no tolerance for "blasphemous" popular music. The one time that Gramps overheard young Wilson singing the innocuous lyrics to a hit Louis Jordan jump tune ("Ain't nobody here but us chickens…"), he promptly whacked the future soul star across the head with a Bible—an unabridged King James version, according to Pickett. The Wicked Pickett would later break into music as a gospel singer.

Return of the Prodigal Son

When New York–based Atlantic Records flew Pickett to a small studio in Muscle Shoals, Alabama, in 1966 for the recording session that produced "Land of 1,000 Dances," it was a pivotal moment in the development of soul. Atlantic had been recording its artists at tiny Stax Records in Memphis, Tennessee, using the house band, Booker T. and the MGs. But they were seeking an even deeper link to the South, and figured Alabama native Pickett would thrive recording in his home state. Pickett, however, had lived in Detroit since he was a teen, and was by then about as Southern as a frozen lake. Jarred when he saw day laborers picking cotton around the tiny airport, the singer was even more surprised to find that Muscle Shoals producer Rick Hall was not black. He got over it, then went to work, where his screaming vocals found a perfect counterpart in the studio's booming horn section. That first Pickett session at Muscle Shoals helped establish the style known as Southern soul, which was looser and more earthy than the Motown sound.

Dancing in the Street

Motown

Martha & the Vandellas

Like a soulful schoolteacher raising her voice above a din of restless horns, Martha Reeves belts out a musical geography lesson in "Dancing in the Street." A No. 2 hit in the summer of '64, "Dancing in the Street" had American teens footloose along the boulevards—and not just in the many cities named in the song. Anticipating the carefree attitude of the '60s, the song became an anthem for letting it all hang out. At the same time, it was wholesome enough to become a Top 40 radio staple. A single from the *Dance Party* album, it has become a perennial party favorite.

The Sound of Young America

Motown founder Berry Gordy's dream of creating "the sound of young America" had become reality by the time "Dancing in the Street" was released. The label, then only five years old (original offices, pictured right), issued 60 singles that year, with 19 of them Top 10 hits. Berry, who once worked at General Motors, ran the company like a factory—employing virtual assembly lines of songwriters, producers and arrangers who cranked out the signature sound. By 1964, the Motortown Revues, as Gordy's caravans were known, were performing to large crowds throughout the country.

She Took Notes

Martha Reeves began working as a secretary at Motown in 1959, a few years after finishing high school. An aspiring vocalist, her big break came when a Motown backup singer fell ill before a recording session and Reeves (below, right) was asked to fill in. Motown producers instantly

recognized her talent, and in 1962 she teamed with Annette Sterling (not pictured) and Rosalind Ashford (above, left) to form the Vandellas. The group sang backup on Marvin Gaye's "Stubborn Kind of Fellow" and "Hitch Hike." A year later, they had a No. 1 R&B hit with "Heat Wave." Betty Kelly (above, center) replaced Sterling in 1964, the year "Dancing" hit the streets.

Dance Fever

"Dancing in the Street" was inspired by a run of dance songs in the early 1960s that included "Bristol Stomp" by the Dovells; a remake of Hank Ballard's "The Twist" by Chubby Checker; "Limbo Rock," also from Checker; Little Eva's "Loco-Motion"; "Walking the Dog" by Rufus Thomas; "C'mon and Swim" by Bobby Freeman; and "Twist and Shout," a hit for the Isley Brothers in 1962 and an even bigger hit for the Beatles in 1964. Motown was happy to ride in on the coattails of the trend with "Dancing in the Street." But by celebrating dancing in general—as opposed to specific dance moves that would inevitably fall out of fashion—the song became the most enduring of the genre. In 1985, Mick Jagger and David Bowie released a version of the song that hit the pop Top 20.

A Brand-New Beat

Motown executive Mickey Stevenson encouraged his secretary Reeves to record, but he struggled to find the right vehicles for her. "Dancing in the Street" was written with established singers Mary Wells and Kim Weston in mind. Still, the Vandellas insisted they should get a crack at it. Stevenson agreed to try, and the song became their biggest hit ever—and their only million-seller. Although the act broke up in 1969, the trio was inducted into the Rock and Roll Hall of Fame in 1995.

Credits and Acknowledgements

Picture Credits

Cover/Title & Contents/IBC: Corbis
Page 2: (TL) Corbis, (BR) FPG International, LLC.
Page 3: (CL) Showtime Archives, (CR) Michael Ochs Archives, (B) Showtime Archives **Page 4:** (TL) Frank Driggs Collection, (BR) Michael Ochs Archives **Page 5:** (CL) Frank Driggs Collection, (TR) Showtime Archives **Page 6:** Archive Photos/Metronome Collection, (BR) Photofest **Page 7:** (TL) Archive Photos/Frank Driggs Collection, (C) Michael Ochs Archives, (BR) FDR/Michael Ochs Archives **Page 8:** (TL) Michael Ochs Archives, (BR) Showtime Archives **Page 9:** (ALL) Showtime Archives **Page 10:** (ALL) Michael Ochs Archives **Page 11:** (CT & CB) Michael Ochs Archives, (CR) Showtime Archives **Page 12:** (TL & BR) Showtime Archives **Page 13:** (CL) Showtime Archives, (CB) Frank Driggs Collection (Charles B. Nadell), (BR) Showtime Archives (Lynne Beale) **Page 14:** (TR) Showtime Archives (Bill Smith), (BL) Archive Photos (Fred G. Korth) **Page 15:** (BL) Showtime Archives, (C) Photofest, (BR) Showtime Archives **Page 16:** (TL) Reproduced from the Collections of the Library of Congress, (BR) Showtime Archives (Curtis Tillman/Andy Grigg) **Page 17:** (TL & BC) Michael Ochs Archives, (CR) London Features International, Ltd.

Page 18: (TL) Archive Photos, (BR) Showtime Archives
Page 19: (CL) Showtime Archives, (TR) Michael Ochs Archives (Colin Escott), (BR) Michael Ochs Archives (Jon Sievert) **Page 20:** (TL) Archive Photos, (BR) PNI **Page 21:** (CL) Corbis, (TR & BR) Showtime Archives **Page 22:** (TL & BR) Michael Ochs Archives (FDR) **Page 23:** (ALL) Michael Ochs Archives **Page 24:** (TL) Michael Ochs Archives, (BR) Showtime Archives (Dave Booth) **Page 25:** (CL) Showtime Archives, (BC & TR) Michael Ochs Archives **Page 26:** (TL) Globe Photos, (BR) Michael Ochs Archives **Page 27:** (TL & BR) Michael Ochs Archives **Page 28:** (TL) AP/Wide World Photos, (BR) Michael Ochs Archives **Page 29:** (CL) Retna Ltd. (David Redfern), (CR) Michael Ochs Archives, (BR) Showtime Archives

The Publisher has made every effort to obtain the copyright holders' permission for the use of the pictures which have been supplied by the sources listed above, and undertakes to rectify any accidental omissions.